YOU HAVE REAL ESTATE IN YOU

THE SIMPLIFIED REAL ESTATE GUIDE TO HELPING YOU UNDERSTAND REAL ESTATE, HOW IT WORKS, AND HOW YOU CAN LEARN AND PROFIT FROM IT.

Davielier Turner

FOREWORD

Have you always been curious about real estate and how it works??

Have you ever thought about getting into real estate and didn't know where to start? Have you heard that it takes a lot of money to start, and you decided to give up before you started? You Have Real Estate in You is loaded with information to help you understand real estate, what it entails, and how you can learn and profit from it.

You will learn:

- Where to get funding and which loan to choose
- What aspect of real estate you want
- That it does not take a lot of money to get involved

- Where to locate your deals
- How to turn your real estate idea into profit

CONTENTS

INTRODUCTION

First, I want to thank you for taking the time to pick up a copy of my book. I've been putting this together for a while, and I hope it will give you some insight into getting started in real estate. I hope that when you finish the book, you will make money in real estate as it changes your understanding of the subject matter for the better. I started writing this book five times and stopped because I wanted to make sure it was understandable and could help create your real estate future. I realized that it must be written.

Real Estate is my passion. It has allowed me to help hundreds of people live their dream as homeowners, investors, flippers, and landlords. It has also allowed me to live freely and make my own schedule, travel when I want to, and support my family.

Now my job is to pass my knowledge on to you so that you will not make the same mistakes that I have done.

Let my failures help you prevent your own. I will share some information that I have learned over my 20 plus years of working in the real estate industry. I hope that the information that I share will help you grow as a dedicated investor, realtor, landlord or just give you a broader knowledge of what real estate is so that you will understand that 'There is Real Estate In You."

This book is dedicated to everyone that has seen me grow from a new real estate agent until now. I appreciate you for believing in me and allowing me to work with and for you. This success is ours, and we all shall continue to win and succeed.

PART ONE

Real Estate Can Not be lost or stolen, nor can it be carried away. Purchased with common sense, paid for in full, and managed with reasonable care, it is about the safest investment in the world.

FRANKLIN D. ROOSEVELT

ONE

WHAT IS REAL ESTATE

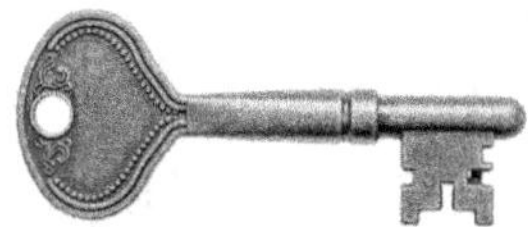

Before we get started, I want to go over some stuff so that you will really understand what the word real estate really consists of. Many people think it's just houses and buildings, but there are many things that real estate consists of.

Real Estate is real property and everything attached to it.

Let's break it down; real property is the house, porch, windows, floors walls. Everything is attached to it, including trees, shrubs, streams, land, lakes. If it is attached to your property, it is real property.

To understand Real Estate, House flipping, renting, wholesaling, one must first understand real property.

Once understood, we break down the functions of different positions in it. Selling involves different functions.

Listing agents — one who lists the property for sellers, putting it on the market and all the multiple listing services as a way to have the property sold for the seller. For this, a real estate license is needed. Selling or Buyers agent — one who brings a buyer to the seller's agent. This is the one you see out showing houses to their clients. A real estate license is also needed. Wholesaler – one who locate properties from sellers and sell or assign to another party. No real estate license is needed for this.
Flipper — One who buys properties at a discount, renovate them, and sell for the current market value. No license is needed if you are selling your personal property. Landlord — one who buys a property and rent it out for a profit; a lot of people do this for additional income.
Buyer — a person who buys a property to become a flipper, a landlord, a wholesaler, or just to live in it.

Determining what aspect of real estate you want to be is up to you.

TWO

REAL ESTATE LICENSE

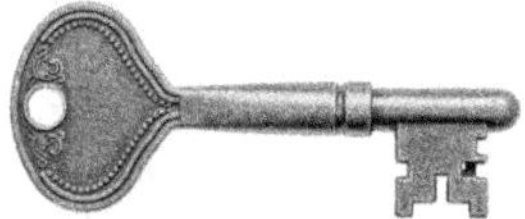

There are many ways to deal with Real Estate and plenty of resources. But to do certain functions, you will be required to have a real estate license in the state you are doing business in. To buy and sell property for other people, a real estate license is required. Now all functions of real estate do not require one, but this one does. Having a license is also a good thing because it allows you to perform as an agent and get a look at the MLS (multiple listing system) before anyone else,

This is where agents put their listings up that they are selling for their clients. This also serves as great information if you are a personal investor or just selling to other investors. I will break down a few different things for you now.

To give real service you must add something which cannot be bought or measured with money, and that is sincerity and integrity.

DOUGLAS ADAMS

THREE
LISTING AGENT

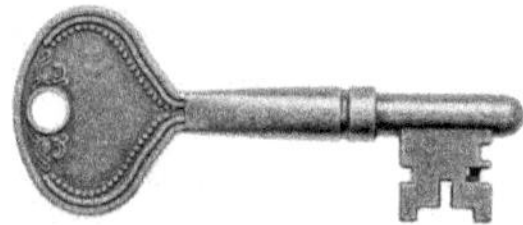

A LISTING AGENT IS A LICENSED REAL ESTATE AGENT that specializes in getting listings from homeowners to sell for them. These agents are the ones that sellers hire to get their homes sold, so they seek out sellers with a track record of getting the homes for them. They are also the ones who get the listings, assist the seller with the listing price and get the commission for selling the listing. They also control the commission split the selling agent or buyer's agent will receive for selling their listing. For example, suppose the listing agent negotiates a 6% commission with the seller. In that case, that does not necessarily mean that the buyer's agent will receive a 3% commission. Some people will think it's only fair to get half, as they came with the buyer. But we consider that the listing agent might have paid for the lead for the listing; they also have fees depending on their marketing. So, most listing agents might offer 2.5% or even 2% when the market is moving, aka a sellers' market (seller market = more buyers than seller). If the market typically slows down and becomes a buyers' market (buyer's market= more sellers than buyers), you will see listing agents more willing to give a 3% commission with a listing deduction fee that could range from $25-$300. But the most simple and plain way to explain this is that the agent who gets the listing controls the commission splits to the other agents. You can list the property, sit back and let another agent sell it, and you still get paid and control what the buyer's agent gets paid. Trust me, you do you want to be the listing agent!

Buyer's Agent- A realtor is not a salesperson; they're a matchmaker. They introduce people to homes until they fall in love with one. Then they're a wedding planner.

FOUR

BUYERS' AGENTS

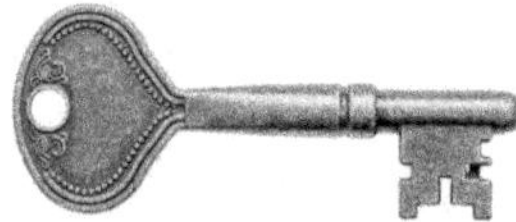

This is the agent that knocks on your door to show your house or apartment when you are selling it or when the landlord is selling it. This agent really does the most work out of all the real estate agents. They Show multiple houses daily. Also, this is the agent that connects most with their clients. This is the agent; if connected right, the buyer will remember them and become the buyer's listing agent in the future. Being on the buyer's agent side over the years, I have gained some great friendships. I have become the go-to agent for many families. This is a real position to upgrade your real estate future position. So, make sure you give your best because one client can become 40 clients, and some clients have very large families. This is also a hard-working position because you could be showing a client forty to one hundred houses. It can really get frustrating but remember this is the biggest purchase of a buyer's life, so some are just waiting for the right property to speak to them. We must remember that they are buying, not us, so what we love for them as their agent they may not. Also, make sure you go over all your client's wants and needs as this will help prevent unnecessary house showing. Once you identify their wants, needs, and location, it makes it just a little easier to find their dream home. Ask them what their must-haves and what spaces in the house are the most important and what they can live without. This helps locate the property a little easier. Also, try to get them to narrow down their search to three areas so that you will not be running all over. A client that says anywhere is good will be harder to get them to concentrate on an area, and you will be running all over. Focusing on three areas assists them with deciding a little easier, and it really helps the both of you.

Also, one of the biggest things is knowing when to fire a client. As an agent, you will not be a perfect match for every client, and they will not be a perfect match for you.

No one wants to fire a client, but there are times that you have to. For example;

1. If they consistently underbid properties when it is sellers' market (sellers' market is when sellers demand top dollar because the prices are up and there is a lack of inventory). Most buyers watch HGTV and really think that's how the process works
2. You showed 30 houses and five were nice and just what they were looking for, but they never

even made one offer on any properties. A friend of mine used to say, "Guess what, I think they just want to hang out with you."

3. Or if you get this line, "oh, my father or friend said when they purchased this, and that happened, and they got the seller down twenty grand and got the closing costs paid by the seller." News flash, this is not back then, and Real Estate Markets change. I can keep going on, but you get the point. Excuses with no real action. I came up with a method years ago that I don't drive anyone around in my car because if you are not serious about buying, I will make sure you waste just as much gas and toll money as I did. It's funny cause you are reading it but trust me, it adds up after a while. People forget realtors do not get paid if they do not close the deal.

Wholesaler- let us never negotiate out of fear but let us never fear to negotiate.

JOHN F. KENNEDY

FIVE

WHAT IS WHOLESALING?

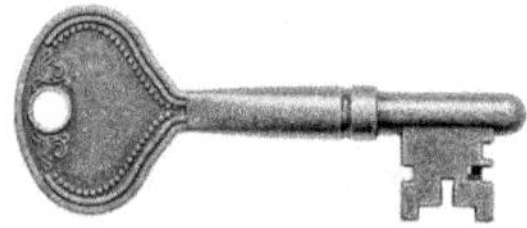

WHOLESALING IS WHEN YOU MAKE MONEY OFF other people's real estate without actually purchasing and closing on it. Thus, as an wholesaler, you are in contract with equitable interest. A wholesaler looks for deals they can sell to an investor who wants to buy the property for long-term rental gains or just a quick fix and flip. Wholesalers contact property owners and ask them if they would like to sell their properties. They scout neighborhoods for vacant properties, for sale by owners, probate clients, tax liens or pre-foreclosures! Some even door knock. Ran down properties are more of the target because the seller can't keep up the upkeep and may just be looking to get out of it. First, they will contact the owner; then, they will put the property under contract for the agreed amount. They lock them in with the binding contract so that they cannot sell it to anyone else. Once that is done, the wholesaler gains control over the property. Then they will go find another buyer to whom they can assign the contract to close the deal. Once that is done, they will be paid a fee that they and the new buyer agreed on. For example, the seller agreed to sell a wholesaler a house at $70,000, then the wholesaler finds a new buyer to purchase it at $88,000. The new buyer knows if they put $20,000 in it, it will be worth $140,000, and just like that, the wholesaler has flipped the contract and made an $18,000 profit. But wholesalers have to hustle to get properties and build a good list of buyers to sign the contract and close within agreed terms they made with the seller. If they don't close within the agreed terms of the contract, the seller can rescind the contract, and it will become null and void.

I have had situations where I wholesaled a property a buyer promised a certain amount for, and they didn't pay that amount but tried to pay way less. So, you have to be very careful when wholesaling. There are some slicksters, so you must align yourself with a good team to make sure that you get paid. As most wholesalers are not licensed, it is hard to bring the case to court and sue for payment.

There are also good and bad points about wholesaling.

The Good

- Very minimal funds needed
- Quick money
- Can do anywhere and no license required
- A good way to build up capital

The Bad

- It offers a one-time pay
- No tax deductions
- Hoping the buyer closes on time or you might lose the deal.
- You are only as good as your last deal.

Buy land, they aren't making it anymore.

MARK TWAIN

SIX

FLIPPING PROPERTIES

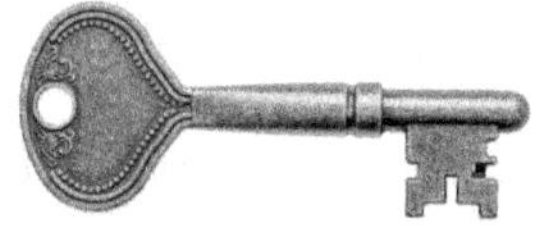

MANY PEOPLE HEAR FLIPPING PROPERTIES, AND THE first thing that comes to their mind is that someone is making a lot of money. Different flips have different after-repair values (ARVs). Trust me, when I first started, I thought I would make a killing, but I was extremely wrong because I did not research what flipping really meant. I remember purchasing a property and rehabilitating it, but once it was finished, I realized that everybody had made more money than me. Now, I'm like, "how is this possible? I was supposed to have gotten rich off this one house." That was my thinking. I did my final numbers and saw that the electrician, the plumber, the sheet rocker, the kitchen crew, and everyone else had made more money than me on my own project. I'm the person who put up the money, paid for and funded the flip. Luckily, I did not lose, but I know that after four months of rehab and putting out thousands of dollars, I was supposed to make more than $8000 profit. There is no way in the world of flipping that $8000 is enough for all the time and effort that was put in. So, in all reality, I lost because, in four months, I only made $8000, and that's because I did not know the pros and cons of flipping. I let everyone take advantage of me because I did not have the knowledge.

With the act of rehabbing or flipping, you have many different fees or, in simple terms, people digging in your pockets. The main things to understand are your numbers and the costs of everything.

The first is the cost to purchase the property, the second is the rehab budget (how much money will it cost to get this house nice and livable again).

The third is the holding cost. During renovation, how much will it cost me monthly until the project is done? Examples include taxes, security gates, light bills, water bills, insurance. The longer it takes, the more holding costs you will pay, and these numbers can add up very quickly.

Then you will finally get to the profit. That's the amount after all your expenses is paid. I don't mean to scare anyone; I just like to give the real effect of flipping. The eye-opening part but the end justifies the means in the profit is the most important part. Like I said in the example before, I only made an $8000 profit, so you have to really decide what profit line you have to make for each property for flipping them to make sense.

Don't be afraid to pass up properties and opportunities because all aren't positive cash flow opportunities. The most important part of flipping is understanding what to buy, when to buy, where to buy, and why the property makes sense to buy. Understanding these four points is the most important.

But before you start, make sure that you have a well-qualified construction team to do the work. Jumping from contractor to contracted can be very costly because although we know our price to pay for something, some contractors have different prices. Get one on your team and build with them from there. Provide them with that system that works well for both of you, and It will get you the best prices they can give you. Create a great partnership with all your contractors. This will save you plenty of headaches and give you more time for yourself. Time is money, and time used renovating and running back and forth to Lowes or Home Depot can be used to find your next deal or next dollar, depending on what it is that you do.

Landlords- "landlords grow rich in their sleep."

UNKNOWN

SEVEN

TO BE A LANDLORD (INVESTING FOR CASH FLOW)

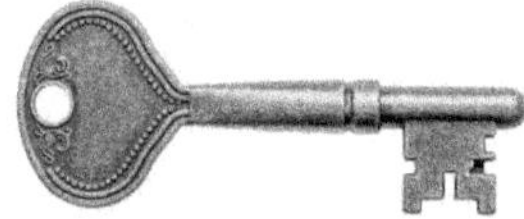

Some people flip properties to sell, and some flip properties to hold. By becoming the landlord, you can create a stable monthly income from holding your properties. For example, you buy a multifamily house and charge to rent the units. Your first floor pays you $1600 a month, and your second floor pays you $2200 a month. Ex. The amount of your monthly mortgage is $2500 with all expenses included water, taxes, insurance. That leaves a monthly profit of $1300 after all expenses are paid. Now purchase multiple properties; let's just say 5, for example. Those will bring $6500 net income to your household a month. You will have a decent amount of monthly income coming in. This is casual investing in real estate. At the same time, it's also wealth creation. I just say five properties, but the more doors you invest, the more money you will have if done correctly. Although all monthly profits on each unit will not be the same, you also have to create a profit point, and that's knowing how much each house has to make after the expenses are paid for to make sense to keep and rent. For example, if I buy this house, I need to make $700 a month profit after all expenses is paid. You have to give yourself a good profit margin because houses make money as well as cost money. Things break in the property and need to be repaired immediately. If the heat is down in the winter, it will need to be repaired ASAP. If the repair cost is $1000, you have already lost over a month's profit. Now just imagine this happening on different properties simultaneously; this can cause real financial distress. That's why your monthly profit number must make the most sense. If it makes profit, it is an "asset," but if it doesn't, it becomes a "liability." The worst thing you can do is lose money while someone else is living comfortably on your dime.

Being a landlord has its pros and cons!

PRO

If you get a good tenant, you will most likely only hear from them during rent collection time. Some tenants will take care of your property like it is their own. Once you get a good tenant, most landlords do their best to try to keep them happy. Although he knows that sometimes, business is business; still, you do not want to run a good tenant away. Every rent increase does not have to be increased, meaning you do not have to raise the rent every year. Even if can raise it up by 3%. Some just can't afford it and to lose a good tenant is very hard. Remember, I'm telling you stuff that I have been through so that you do not have to go through it. One time I raised the rent on a good tenant in my beginning years and ran the tenant off. It took me seven tenants and five years later to get another good tenant. I was evicting and going back and forth to court for the tenants for months. I can honestly say I made the wrong decision by running away from the good stable tenant over a $75 rate increase, and it cost me thousands and a few years to get it back right.

CON

The cons of a bad tenant are that it can cost you thousands of dollars and total loss of good tenants. I once had a good tenant on the first floor quiet who stayed to themselves. I rented the second unit out to a client with three teenage boys who blasted music all day and night inside the house and made outside the house their hangout spot. Now, remember I had a nice couple downstairs that was quiet and respectable. This noisy group ran them away, and they decided to move. So, you have to be careful, or you will lose good tenants just as I did. It's very important to match energy with tenants. Another con is that you have to take them to court for payment and eviction when they do not pay, which costs time, money, filing fees, and attorney fees. A day is a lot to lose, running back and forth to court. That is time and money that you will never recoup. Some states like New Jersey are easy on the tenants and you will really have to fight for your payment or your property back and, in some cases, be going back and forth of the court for years, and that's a lot of profit lost.

Now I remember even though your tenant is not paying, you are still responsible for the mortgage, taxes, and insurance. Regardless so they can really become a financial burden on someone that is literally just making it. So, tenant screening is very important. Some landlords ask for a credit report before renting. Some also ask for a national tenant network (NTN).

This report tells you if the tenants have any private evictions, liens, or judgments against them. It also gives a number on the report to say where their credit score might be. These reports really help you to screen your tenants. Another important thing is to include all of the expectations and exemptions in your lease. Some just go and buy a standard staples lease. Although it is a good lease, there are more things that you could put in a lease to protect you. You want the tenants to know the penalty for paying late because if this is not highlighted, the tenants will pay you when they want. For example, rent is due on or before the fifth of every month; if payment is late from the fifth to the 10th, a $50 late fee will be added. If payment is received from the 10th to the 15th, there will be an additional late fee charge of $150. You can also let them know how many people are allowed to be living on the premises. If washers and dryers are allowed, if the parking is free or has a monthly charge. You can stipulate the terms in your lease. Trust me, this will save you a lot of headaches if you do this. Especially if you take them to court for eviction on any of the terms listed above.

But as I said, it has its pros and cons but can be lucrative for long-term gains and extra funds for the long term.

Sometimes you will hear people say that their goal is to own a certain number of doors. Well, that means only a number of rental units. They are great rental income if they make financial sense. Like, what's the use of owning a bunch of doors if none of them are making any real profit. For example, you own a two-family house, "2 doors," but you only make $200 a month off each unit after all the bills are paid. $200 is nothing if things start to break. One furnace breaks and the cost to repair is $1,400, it will take you 7 months to recoup the furnace money back. So that's 7 months of no profit, hoping that nothing else breaks down. That's why it's very important for your rental units to make the most financial sense. Owning doors is good if you have a target number (that makes sense) that you need to make off each. I'm in New Jersey, and the prices are up as well as the cost of living, so the rents are high. This market will be different from a south market where the houses prices are lower. Hence, doors and rental income will depend on the state and market that you are in. Currently, right now in 2021, the interest rates are low, so your price per door will change depending on location. So, make sure your price per door makes financial sense, or you will have negative profit and end up what people call house poor.

Real estate investing even on a very small scale, remains a tried-and-true means of building an individual's cash flow and wealth.

ROBERT KIYOSAKI

EIGHT

COMMERCIAL REAL ESTATE

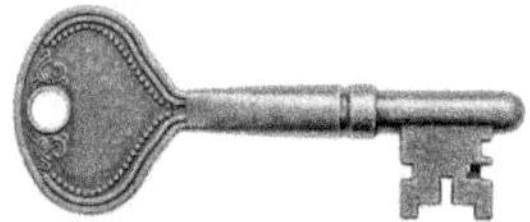

THE DIFFERENCE BETWEEN RESIDENTIAL REAL estate and commercial real estate is that instead of one to four family rental houses, you can deal with office buildings, churches, gas stations, theaters, food stores, shopping malls with various stores, hotels, movie theaters, laundromats, etc.

Once again, you do not need a license to do these if you are doing them for yourself, but if you sell for someone, then you will. Commercial is a big deal and will require expertise, but it is also no different from residential investing. The only difference is there is an opportunity to make more money.

The biggest difference is its lending practices. The bank usually requires a 20% to 30% down payment depending on experience and assets.

They are also not backed by the government, so the bank has different guidelines. They want a big down payment for security purposes. In Real Estate, we call this "skin in the game." With a bigger down payment, you are less likely to walk away from the property because you are strongly invested in it. Also, the property numbers must make sense so that the bank will see that there is room for the monthly mortgage to get paid.

Also, as an agent doing commercial real estate, you are allowed to name your commission. Whereas with residential, you will see most commissions start at 6%. Still, with commercial real estate, I have seen brokers make as much as 10% commission to sell. It's like having a name your price tool for real estate. But you must have experience in that field.

You can't buy happiness, but you can buy real estate, and that's kind of the same thing.

UNKNOWN

NINE

RESIDENTIAL REAL ESTATE

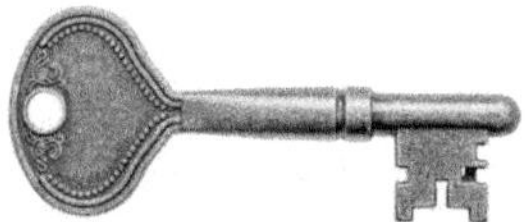

Residential real estate is simple. It's basically property with one of four units. Some people use them for rental investments and some to simply live in. The good thing about residential real estate is that you can purchase with little or no money down. And the reason is most loans are government-backed. FHA, VA, conventional are all government-backed loans. Some require private mortgage insurance (PMI); some say mortgage insurance premium (MIP). VA is backed by the government through the department of veteran affairs. They back and assist first-time homeowners.

FHA Loan — 3.5% down
Conventional Loan — 5% down
VA Loan — 0% down

These government back loans make it easier for first-time homeowners to purchase a place to call home.

One more thing about residential real estate.

Condos and co-ops have additional maintenance fees. Some are FHA-approved, and some are not. If a condo is not FHA-approved, then you might have to go conventional and put a higher down payment down. Because the building or the management company did not meet the requirements for the property to be on the FHA-approved list.

One of the best things about residential real estate is that it can help start your investment portfolio. If you buy a four-family property first, then a year later, you can buy a two-family or one-family without having to put 20 to 25% down. This is considered an upgrade. It's best to do it this way because the multi-family unit could pay for your single-family unit if the rent rolls are good. But I know some people that just don't like people, so some just buy the one family first and relax. But if you buy a one-family first and then go for a multifamily later, they will consider you an investor, and your down payment will be 20% to 25%. That's why I suggest grabbing the multifamily first then going to the one family later. It enables investment with less money down and helps with becoming an investor faster.

Don't wait to buy real estate, buy real estate, and wait.

T HARV EKER

TEN

DEVELOPMENT

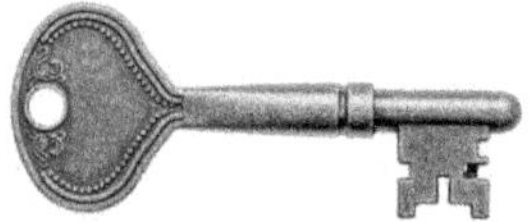

ONCE YOU START MAKING MONEY AND RUBBING shoulders with the big wigs, then residential and commercial real estate becomes boring, at least that's what the rich say (I don't know yet; that's why I'm still here writing books. But one day, I will find out. But let's just say, for now, life is great). But development is a business process, encompassing activities that range from the renovation and the release of existing buildings to the purchase of real land and the sale of developed land or parcels. All these activities come from ideas that convert from paper to real property. Although many developers also manage the construction process or engage in house building, it's different from construction or house building.

Developers buy land, finance real estate deals, build or have other builders build projects, create imagined control, and orchestrate the process of development from beginning till the end. Developers usually take the greatest risk in the creation or renovation of real estate and receive the greatest rewards. Typically, the purchase price of a parcel or tract of land determines the marketing of the property. They develop the building program and design, obtain the necessary approvals and financing, build the structures, and decide if they want to keep or sell them.

Sometimes property developers will only do part of the process. For example, some source for a property and create the plans and permits approved before selling the property with the plans and permits to a builder at a premium price. Ultimately, a developer who is also a builder may purchase a property with the plans and permits in place so they do not risk failing to obtain plan approval and can start the construction or the development immediately. Developers work with many different divisions—architects, city planners, engineers, surveyors, inspectors, contractors, lawyers, leasing agents, etc. So, as you can see, there is a lot to developing, which is why the reward is great; however, you will encounter headaches first. I suggest you start building single and multifamily units first, then move on to the big major development projects.

Most people…find a disorientating mismatch between the long-term nature of their liabilities and the increasingly short-term nature of their assets.

JAMES BALDWIN

ELEVEN

ASSET VERSUS LIABILITY MYTH

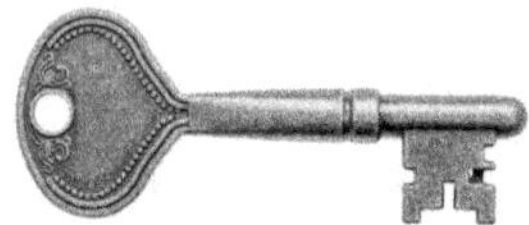

Assets are those items that can be transformed into cash or that generate income over time. Liabilities are obligations that most pay for simple and plain

Houses are both depending on usage. If you have multi-family houses and rent the units out, and it pays for itself and make profit, you have an asset. Also, if the property is backed by a small mortgage and you can refinance and take some of the equity out for future investments, then you, my friend, have an asset. But let's say you only own a two-family house, and you are working hard every day just to pay your mortgage and bills; then, your house will be considered a liability. When there is no stream of income coming in from it, the property is just a liability. So, when people say that a home is an asset, it can really go both ways. The way you use yours will determine which one it is. But if you can pay it off or down and have equity in it, it can become an asset.

BEFORE

AFTER

BEFORE

AFTER

BEFORE

AFTER

BEFORE

AFTER

PART TWO

You do not get what you want. You get what you negotiate.

HARVEY MACKAY

TWELVE

NEGOTIATION

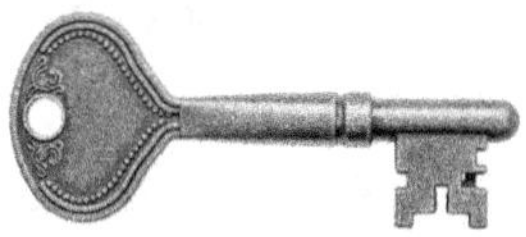

One of the main things we see every day in person and in real life is negotiation. If they get their price, you get your price, both of you meet in the middle, but either way, to agree on terms, someone excepted a price and got to the price.

NEGOTIATION POINTS

- Have a good attitude and let the other side warm up and feel comfortable
- Take your game face-off, the smile goes further
- Always try to negotiate face-to-face; it's always best to look at a person, and one will either whimper, weaken or gain a natural respect
- Always watch your body language, a comfortable view is always best, and it helps take a guard down

- Find common ground for a meeting in the middle. Anything to warm up the moment
- Do not become emotionally attached to the deal because it can only hurt you in the long run. Remember, there is always a deal waiting, and you just have to find it.
- Show that you have a sense of humor when the moment hits
- Always end the negotiation on a good note; even if you don't get the deal, you can get an ally
- Never act excited then they will be harder to negotiate with because they know you're very interested
- Knowledge is power. The more you know, the more professional you sound to them, and they will not be able to run over you
- Let them think they're running the show; let them speak first. That way, they think they are in control when they really are not.
- Know your business so that way you can have an answer for every question. Once you start looking lost, you have lost the edge.

Some agents are very aggressive and experienced negotiators, and that's why some get hired for their services. Once you learn negotiation, that's half of the system.

I wish I could buy you for what you are worth and sell you for what you think you're worth. I sure would make money on the deal.

ZORA NEALE HURSTON

THIRTEEN

IS THE DEAL WORTH IT?

No matter which way you choose to do real estate, the deal has to make sense. If it's flipping, wholesaling, listing, or selling, it just has to make sense.

- Know your price point and your market; you do not want to overpay for any deal. Knowing your market is knowing what it's worth now, what it's worth in six months and even next year.
- Do you have room for a major renovation or a patch job?

For some deals, you can get away with a patch job, while others may require the full renovation. You have to learn the numbers of what everything costs you. Once you learn the numbers, you have to have a budget to keep your future profit lined up. For years I have seen many newcomers to flipping properties start to design projects like they were going to live there. It's great to put out a nice product, but it's bad to overdo it and weaken your budget. We have to remember if flipping that the sale number justifies the means if it is worth it. Don't buy or renovate with your heart. Each house is just that—a house.

Even if you are listing a property for a seller, you have to ask what price they have in mind to sell it, then give them comparable explaining the numbers in their area. Some sellers have overboard expectations, and some have overappreciated their homes in the area that does not sell for the price that they want. For example, all the houses in your area are similar and sell for $180,000. But you did a $220,000 renovation on yours, and now, you want to sell for $400,000. This is the meaning of over appreciating. This is the real "is the listing worth its scenario?" I'm not saying that it will never sell, but I'm saying it will be almost impossible to sell.

So, always ask, is this deal worth it? Is listing worth it, or is the client worth dealing with?

If you don't take care of your customer, your competitor will.

BOB HOOEY

FOURTEEN
NEGOTIATING FOR SELLERS OR BUYERS

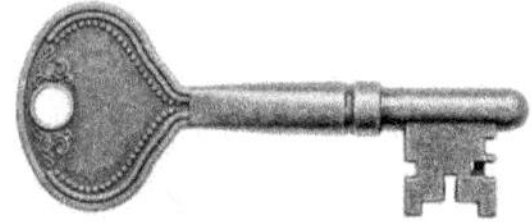

One of the hardest things a seller can hear is that their house is not worth all the mortgage payments, pain, sweat, and tears that they have put into it over the years. Everyone has a price in their mind, even if it's not realistic. Still, no matter what price people have in their heads, the area comparable within the last six months will dictate the price. Let's just say give or take, a few dollars added or subtracted for bathrooms, garages, etc. Houses with two bathrooms might be worth several more thousand than a house with one bathroom. A house with a garage might be worth $3000 more than a house without one. Hence, as a realtor, wholesaler, or flipper, one must know these things when speaking to the seller. Also, it's always a great idea to bring about five comparable to a seller when you are trying to get the listing. "They say men lie, women lie, but numbers don't."

As for the buyers, all buyers want a property for less or to negotiate. We also have to be stern or honest with the buyers. One of the most logical lines that always work for me with buyers is, "if that was your house that you are selling would you be happy with that offer." It throws it back on the buyer and brings them back to his sense of reality. But we also want to get them the best deal possible because if you are their agent, it makes you look like the good guy and you do work for them. But negotiations are never as simple. Some people watch reality shows and believe that they can see three properties, make a lowball offer, and have the owner accept it. Or the I'm paying cash so I can offer what I want. The cash offer is one of the biggest misinterpretations. Although we know cash is king, it doesn't really matter to a person with a mortgage. Some people need their price to move on sale. You will encounter a lot of "I have cash" buyers. Some are serious, and some are full of it. Most of them will be investors, and some regular people will buy cash just to live there. But your job is to simply know your buyer's or seller's needs and get the best deal for them; that is why they hired you.

I will forever believe that buying a home is a great investment. Why? Because you can't live in a stock certificate. You can't live in a mutual fund.

OPRAH WINFREY

FIFTEEN

FUNDING

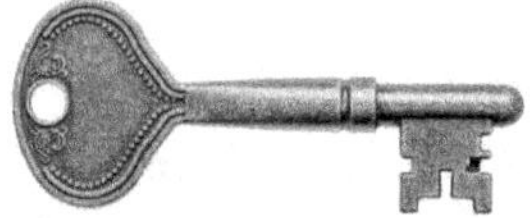

There are so many different funding sources when purchasing units, but I'll get straight to it.

Cash – your own funds come in from your account, family, friends, etc.
Hard money — Short-term money borrowed, which is secured by the real estate that is purchased with it. Most Hard money lenders have a higher interest rate with more liquid required out of your pocket. Most ask for 20% down on your first few deals. They want to make sure that you have some "skin in the game" or money invested. They also have shorter loan terms where a typical loan is 30 years. Most hard money loans are a one-year term, and they are mostly interest-only terms. So, the loan is designed for fix, flip and selling quickly.
Private Money – Investors who lend money for different things. You can negotiate the term and

the rates with them, but most, like hard money, lend short term, so you must have an exit strategy.

FHA loans – loans backed by the federal government and intended for home buyers who are usually not qualified for a mortgage, allowing lower down payment.

Conventional loans – a loan that's not backed by the government and guaranteed to the private sector. It is one of the most used.

VA loan – housing loan backed by the Department of Veterans Affairs for those who have served or currently serve in the US military.

Although there are still more factors of these loans, these are the primary ways home purchases get funded. Depending on what angle you want to go with purchasing, you can always research other resources.

With most of these products, you will deal with a loan officer who will tell you how much you can borrow. But the funding is the most important thing, and it's always good to have lined up before you start property searching. The right mortgage company or person is very essential to this business. I have seen some company's/loan officers give clients a preapproval letter to go out shopping with, and the agent finds them a property, they end up putting one under contract. Next, they do the home inspection, appraisal and all of a sudden, the loan officer tells them later that they do not qualify. This is all because they didn't collect all the necessary paperwork upfront before issuing a pre-approval. The clients are upset, but you are their agent, so you can't assume; you have to ask them upfront if they have submitted all of their documents. The person who is really upset the most is the seller and the seller's agent because that time was wasted and could have been purchased by someone else. Now think, if you have another buyer that's interested in one of the listing agent's ten other listings, do you think they would tell the seller to take your deal? You might have just been blackballed by the agent. That's why it is very important to have the financing in place.

Always make sure your loan officer asks for these documents upfront.

1. Last 2 years tax returns
2. Last 4 paystubs
3. Last 3 months bank statements all accounts
4. Copy of I.D & Social security card

The best thing is to have a very experienced loan officer in your corner, as it will make your life so much easier and make other agents and sellers believe in your craft.

CHECKLIST BY AGENTS OR FLIPPERS

- Always have info to three good real estate attorneys
- Have a relationship with different title

companies as when dealing with hard money, vetting is needed.

- Have a list of appraisers. Some sellers may require an appraisal before they sell the property to you or list it.
- Create a list of reliable home inspectors. When you have a good relationship, they will make time to service your clients and you.
- Have a few options for insurance companies for your clients and yourself.
- Exterminator services for the client.
- Oil tank removal services.

All the services are important because first, in the business, everyone needs them. Second, it makes you seem very knowledgeable to your clients. An agent with all the solutions and information will gain big respect and comfort with their clients. Arm yourself by knowing where to go for information.

PART THREE

"Mindset is what separates the best from the rest."

UNKNOWN

SIXTEEN
MINDSET

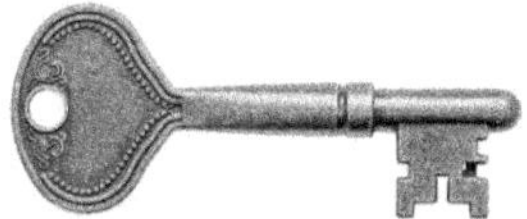

THE MAIN THING ABOUT REAL ESTATE IS TO HAVE the mindset to do it; it is not a get rich quick thing. It takes time to learn and requires consistency with a strong commitment. If you are going to be an agent, it is hard being a part-time agent. I recommend a part-time agency with a team because you might have an appraisal or inspection during your work hours, and you will need someone to assist you. Flipping and investing is easier to do part-time. But most flippers work in some form of real estate or have some type of flexibility in their schedule. Once you lock in and commit, you will see how everything comes together. Remember, there is Real Estate in you. The more committed you are, the more success that you will have. Personally, I eat, sleep, and breathe real estate. That's what I have been doing for 21 years full-time, and I love it, but I had to brace myself and let my mind know that I had to commit and go all-in with it. There was no turning back for me. All in or nothing. For many people, it's hard to commit because they choose a safety net, meaning if this doesn't work in a month, I'm going back to a job. Once you put in your mind that this is all that you have and there is nothing to fall back to, you will succeed because you have to succeed at it.

In life, you have 3 choices: Give up, give in, or give it your all.

CHARLESTON PARKER

SEVENTEEN

GIVING YOUR ALL

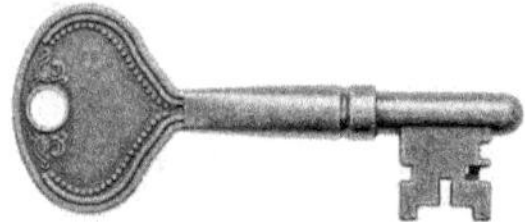

Once you invest in yourself, you have to give it your all. You have to go all-in, no slacking and definitely no damn excuses. Every dollar you invest in this business, you want to gain at least six times that. I see people invest in classes and courses and then stop, quit and just give up. I say to myself they just wasted money. Do you have money to waste? If so, you can give it to me and don't even start. They say only one in seven agents make it to becoming a successful real estate agent. No one can make you a successful agent, flipper, or renovator; it has to be somewhere deep down within yourself. You have to go in there, grab it and bring it out. I can tell you stories of people who quit, and I can also tell you stories of people who reach the top of the chain of success, and you can reach it too; it's up to you. There were times when I felt like giving up initially, but I honestly hated wasting my hard-earned money. So, I had to decide if I worked all those hours just to waste money or invest in myself. A lot of times, people give up because they are doing it all wrong. We have to walk the simple learning steps before we get to the gratification part. Implement a plan on the type of business you want to do and then focus on it

Find time to be alone and focus

- A good clean space, a cluttered space can clutter your thought.
- Shut everything down to focus. We can't be distracted; turn the telephone, TV, and social media off
- Implement what you get from all of this and make it manifest itself

Most successful people succeed by giving their all to what they truly believe in. Amazon started from the garage, and the reason it became so successful is that Mr. and Mrs. Bezos believed in their dream and gave it their all.

Learning the ins and outs- anyone who stops learning is old. Whether at twenty or eighty. Anyone who keeps learning stays young.

HENRY FORD

EIGHTEEN

LEARNING THE INS AND OUTS

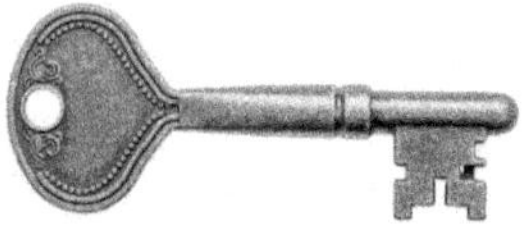

To be successful, one must continue to educate themselves. Education does not stop because we have learned something. There are steps to learning the ins and outs.

1. Consistently ask questions. No question is a dumb question if we are seeking knowledge.
2. The Internet is a tool to learn anything; all of the information is on it. Use it and treat it as a best friend.
3. Get a coach or join a team you can learn as you go
4. Be driven! People gravitate to persons with determination
5. Learn your Market and locations. This is very important people will trust your knowledge.
6. Be willing to go above and beyond people remember who helped them out.
7. Be consistent with people; call and text

> constantly, and they'll remember you. Either they will be annoyed, or the fact that you do Real Estate will be embedded in their mind.

Although there are more things you can do, those are just a few to get you started.

"The victory of success is half won when one gains the habit of setting goals and achieving them."

OG MANDINO

NINETEEN

SETTING GOALS

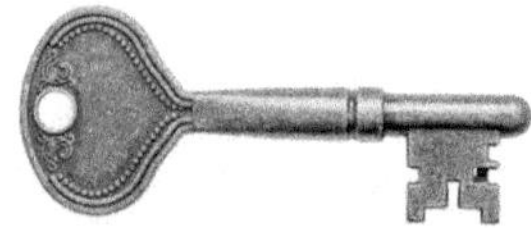

Set Yearly, Monthly, Weekly And Daily Goals

1. If your goal is to cold call 20 people per day, go beyond it and call 25 people.
2. If your goal is to sell 5 million your first year, you can work at it to hit more.
3. Your goal chart will determine your success.
4. Goals are just what we aim for, but once we pass them, success starts.
5. Create a goal chart, set it as your screensaver or sit it by your monitor so that you can look at it daily. The more you see it, the more you will aim to complete it.
6. It's OK to be hard on yourself but do not drown in it. Yes, you want to hit the goals, but if you set 10 realistic goals and only get seven of them, that's a passing grade. 70% of your goal was hit. Now pat yourself on the back; that is an accomplishment

7. Get an accountability partner, as then, you will have each other to push towards the goals.

Remember, setting goals also helps set up a structure, and structure makes hitting your goals easier.

When you want to succeed as bad as you want to breathe, then you will be successful.

ERIC THOMAS

TWENTY

YOU HAVE TO MAKE IT WORK.

When you attack Real Estate, you have to give it your all. Eric Thomas said, "when you want to see as bad as you want to breathe, then you'll be successful."

When I first got started, I said, I can do this and make this work. I attacked it like this was the only thing that I could do or knew how to do. I closed eight deals in my first six months in real estate. I had to go all in and make it happen. There wasn't no turning back for me. My first six months were spent setting up my career; I resigned from my previous job as a Help Desk Tech for an investment firm. In my first six months, I made my whole year salary that I was making as a help desk tech. At that point, I knew what I wanted to do and what I was going to do. I clamped down, networked with mortgage reps, other realtors, and anyone else in the business. It worked for me, and now 20+ years later, I am still enjoying Real Estate and the fruits of its labor. So, for me, it was not a choice; I left my job, so I had to make it work. You have to dedicate certain hours daily and, in a few months, it will work for you.

Don't fear the storm, for the rainbow's never far behind.

JAMIE WORTHINGTON

TWENTY-ONE

THERE IS A RAINBOW AT THE END OF THE TUNNEL

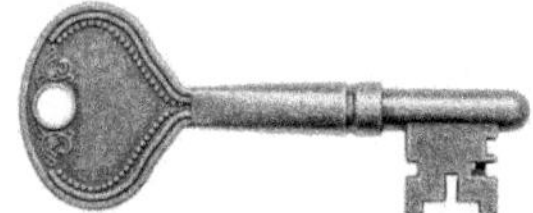

When you work hard to accomplish your goals in real estate, it will definitely become easier. Some of the top agents do not work as hard as they used to because they figured out what systems to implement and what really works for them. If your goal is to flip, learn everything about it—material cost, labor costs, etc., then lay it out on a spreadsheet. If it's wholesale, you must learn where you can target sellers to lock up your deals, sheriff's sales, and foreclosure list probate. If it is to be a realtor, learn all the above plus more. Learn where to locate sellers and buyers use all your resources available. There is a set of New sellers and buyers every day ready to be sold.

One of the biggest jewels I can tell any agent, flipper, or wholesaler.

1. You should know all of your neighbors around

you; they all need to know what it is that you do.

2. Always follow up and return calls as soon as possible, some people are impatient, and business awaits no one.
3. Social media is free marketing and advertising so make sure that you utilize and maximize it.
4. "You do have real estate in you."

ABOUT THE AUTHOR

As a real estate agent with over 20 years of experience, I have taken parts of those 20+ years, good and bad, and put them in this book. I want people to see and understand that it is less difficult than it seems. This book is for experienced professionals, new agents, flippers, landlords, wholesalers, or anyone seeking simple information for their personal use. This book can be a guide to accomplish those goals as well as earn a profit.

Davielier Turner is an established real estate broker in the New Jersey area that has been selling, listing, and flipping real estate for over 20+ years. He is also part owner of Pinnacle Real Estate Group and the sole owner of B.C Enterprises, a company that specializes in flipping properties.

www.ingramcontent.com/pod-product-compliance
Lightning Source LLC
La Vergne TN
LVHW020646100826
845148LV00012B/2353